For over thirty years, the Harvard Institutes for Higher Education (HIHE) have been an important resource for the leadership of colleges and universities. HIHE offers world-renowned professional development programs, providing campus leaders with the information and insights necessary for personal and institutional success. All of these programs incorporate the use of case studies. HIHE regularly produces new case studies, to ensure that its teaching materials reflect the most current issues confronting campus leaders. HIHE maintains the country's largest collection of case studies in higher education administration. These case studies are used in professional development programs and in graduate-level courses in educational administration.

To request information on HIHE's professional development programs or to receive a current catalogue of case studies, please contact Harvard Institutes for Higher Education, 14 Story Street, 4th floor, Cambridge, MA 02138

Teaching Notes to Casebook I

Faculty Employment Policies

James P. Honan and
Cheryl Sternman Rule
with Susan B. Kenyon

JOSSEY-BASS
A Wiley Company
www.josseybass.com

Published by

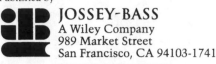

JOSSEY-BASS
A Wiley Company
989 Market Street
San Francisco, CA 94103-1741

www.josseybass.com

Jossey-Bass books and products are available through most bookstores. To contact
Jossey-Bass directly, call (888) 378-2537, fax to (800) 605-2665, or visit our website at
www.josseybass.com.

Substantial discounts on bulk quantities of Jossey-Bass books are available to corpora-
tions, professional associations, and other organizations. For details and discount information, contact the special sales department at Jossey-Bass.

Library of Congress Cataloging-in-Publication Data

Teaching notes to casebook I : faculty employment policies /
James P. Honan and Cheryl Sternman Rule ; with Susan B.
Kenyon.
        p. cm.
Includes bibliographical references.
   ISBN 0-7879-5393-8 (alk. paper)
  1. College personnel management—Study and teaching
(Higher) —United States. 2. College teachers—Employment—United
States. 3. Case method—Study and teaching (Higher)—United
States. I. Title: Teaching notes to casebook one. II. Honan,
James P. III. Rule, Cheryl Sternman. IV. Kenyon, Susan B.
   LB2331.66 .T43 2002
   378.1'2—dc21

2001008649

FIRST EDITION
PB Printing   10 9 8 7 6 5 4 3 2 1

Contents

Preface

The teaching notes contained in this volume are designed to serve as a companion to *Casebook I: Faculty Employment Policies*. This volume provides instructors and discussion leaders with specific advice and suggested approaches to teaching each of the cases in the *Casebook*.

Each teaching note follows a common format and contains the following elements: an outline of the teaching goals of the case and a teaching plan, complete with an introduction, discussion themes, questions for participants, teaching tips, suggested activities, and, finally, a wrap-up section highlighting major learning points with which instructors may choose to conclude their sessions. At the end of each teaching note, we have included the same discussion questions and suggested background readings that appear at the end of the cases themselves. (Two teaching notes—for the Georgia State University and the University of Minnesota cases—also contain case updates. Advice on how to incorporate these updates into the case discussions is provided in the corresponding teaching note.)

Instructors and discussion leaders should be aware that the ideas, advice, and suggestions in the teaching notes are solely jumping-off points to guide the teaching process and to help organize the case discussion. They are merely recommendations, and instructors should, of course, adapt the notes to their own individual styles and preferences and feel free to overlook any suggestions that do not meet the needs of individual discussion groups, classes, workshops, and professional development seminars.

Instructors and discussion leaders who desire more in-depth advice on case-method teaching should consult *Using Cases in Higher Education: A Guide for Faculty and Administrators* in this series.

1

Teaching Note:
Blessed Trinity College
Modifying Faculty Evaluation and Contracts

The Blessed Trinity College (a pseudonym for an actual institution) case can serve as the basis of discussion for a number of important policy issues and challenges, including the modification of faculty evaluation and promotion policies, the role and influence of governance structures in institutional reform efforts, and the leadership requirements for facilitating changes in faculty employment and worklife.

This teaching note is designed to support the instructor using this case. The questions, discussion points, and exercises provided here represent one possible approach to teaching the Blessed Trinity College case. As the instructor gains familiarity with this particular case, he or she will likely adapt the outline according to audience and experience.

Goals

The note is based on the following goals for teaching the Blessed Trinity College case:

This teaching note was prepared for the Project on Faculty Appointments by James P. Honan and Cheryl Sternman Rule and funded by the Pew Charitable Trusts. © 2000 by the President and Fellows of Harvard College.

- To examine the relationship between faculty evaluation policies and the terms and conditions of faculty employment

- To analyze the link between governance structures and processes and institutional reform initiatives regarding faculty worklife

- To identify strategies for facilitating changes in faculty evaluation and employment policies

Teaching Plan

The Blessed Trinity College case highlights several of the difficulties inherent in modifying faculty evaluation and employment policies. The case also illustrates a number of important dilemmas regarding governance that are embedded in policy discussions underway at many campuses throughout the United States. (See Recommended Background Readings at the end of this teaching note, particularly Miller, 1987, and Bess, 1997). Suggested discussion questions to guide participant preparation are included at the end of this teaching note.

Teaching Tip: Since the case focuses heavily on faculty roles and key elements of faculty work, it can be helpful for the instructor to poll participants to assess their general familiarity with these issues. If the case discussion participants consist primarily of faculty or administrators who have had experience as faculty members, this will not be an issue of concern. However, if the participant group is comprised mostly of individuals who have not served as faculty members before, it can be useful to provide an overview of faculty roles and functions and to highlight key faculty governance structures and approaches before delving into the details of the case and the particular dilemmas it raises regarding faculty employment and evaluation.

Discussion

The instructor should plan to organize participant discussion of the Blessed Trinity College case around the following themes:

1. Faculty evaluation policies and the terms and conditions of faculty employment

2. Governance structures, processes, and policy reform

3. Facilitating organizational change: leadership strategies and approaches

The first segment of the discussion deals with the particular issues of faculty evaluation and faculty contract systems; the other two segments focus on the more general issues of governance and organizational change. The instructor can decide which of these perspectives to highlight depending on the overall instructional goals for using the Blessed Trinity College case.

Faculty Evaluation Policies and the Terms and Conditions of Faculty Employment

This segment of the discussion can focus on the policy context within which faculty at Blessed Trinity College are hired, evaluated, and promoted. The instructor can also ask participants to consider what the experience of being a faculty member might be like under the existing evaluation and contract policies at Blessed Trinity College and to consider the changes the new policies might bring. A set of opening questions for this segment might include:

- What is it like to be a faculty member at Blessed Trinity College?

- How do the existing faculty employment and evaluation policies work? Describe some of the key features of faculty worklife that result from these policies.

- What are the goals and purposes of the new evaluation and multiyear contract policies? In what ways will these policies have an impact on the life of faculty at Blessed Trinity? What problems do the new policies appear to solve? What new problems are created by the revised policies?

- Would implementation of the new policies result in a positive outcome for the institution? For the faculty? Why or why not?

Activity: Engage participants in a brief role play activity during this segment of the case discussion. The instructor can ask participants to imagine that they are faculty members at Blessed Trinity College and to address the following questions in groups of two or three people: What would be the biggest changes Blessed Trinity College faculty would experience if the new evaluation and contract policies were implemented? Would these changes be good for the faculty? Good for the institution? After giving the groups five to ten minutes to discuss these questions, the instructor can then engage the entire participant group in a general debriefing of the highlights from the small group discussions, perhaps using a "before and after" or "old policy and new policy" framework for this portion of the conversation.

Governance Structures, Processes, and Policy Reform

This segment of the case discussion examines the link between governance structures and processes and policy reforms in faculty employment and worklife. The instructor can begin by asking participants to create a map of the various players in the Blessed Trinity College governance structure. Among the key players who deserve mention are:

- *The Tenure Study Group.* In what ways is the work of this group helpful to reform efforts regarding faculty life?

- *The Faculty Evaluation Committee*. What are the strengths and weaknesses of this committee's work?

- *The Contracts and Promotion Committee*. What role did the Contracts and Promotion Committee play in the case? Was it effective? Why or why not?

Additional questions include:

- Why haven't the faculty evaluation policies and multi-year contract policies been implemented?

- What are the institutional risks of not implementing these policies? Are there risks to the faculty (individually or collectively)? If so, what are they?

> *Teaching Tip:* To capture fully the complexity and subtlety of some of the key governance problems and challenges embedded in this case, the instructor should allow ample time to encourage participants to describe in detail how the governance processes at the institution do or do not enable reform efforts to move ahead. In addition to an analysis of "who does what," the instructor should also probe participants with questions about "who should do what," so that missed opportunities for progress in implementing the new evaluation and contract policies can be identified and analyzed.

Facilitating Organizational Change:
Leadership Strategies and Approaches

This segment of the case discussion should focus specifically on the dilemmas facing Dean Carol Roberts. The two questions underlying this part of the discussion are: How can an academic leader best encourage and carry out organizational change? and Are there particular leadership strategies or approaches that are more effective than others? In order to address these more general questions through the particular experience of Carol Roberts and her colleagues at Blessed Trinity College, the instructor can pose some or all of the following questions:

- What is your assessment of the overall situation which Carol Roberts has inherited?

- What are the greatest challenges she faces regarding the implementation of the new faculty evaluation and multiyear contract policies?

- What should Carol Roberts do? Why?

- Are there things that she should not do? What risks might she run if she pursues these possible actions?

Activity: Ask participants to imagine themselves serving as consultants to Roberts. Participants can spend five to ten minutes in groups of two to four formulating advice and recommendations for her regarding what she should and should not do to facilitate the implementation of the faculty evaluation and multiyear contract policies. Selected participants can be invited to take part in a brief role playing exercise, with one participant playing the role of Carol Roberts and one or more participants playing the role of consultant. The instructor can debrief the role plays and ask the discussion participants to assess and make sense of the advice that the consultants have offered.

Teaching Tip: Carol Roberts is clearly in a difficult predicament at the end of the Blessed Trinity College case. The instructor should attempt to highlight the full complexity of Roberts' situation and try to push participants to identify the advantages and disadvantages of various leadership approaches and strategies in this segment of the discussion. It can also be helpful to ask participants to identify some of the risks associated with various courses of action that Roberts might take to facilitate the implementation of the new evaluation and contract policies.

Wrap-up: Learning Points and Take-Aways

The instructor can close the discussion of the Blessed Trinity College case by highlighting the following learning points and take-aways:

1. Governance structures and processes play an important role in enabling or preventing innovation. To a certain extent, the very structures and processes designed to foster innovation in faculty employment and worklife can be responsible for impeding progress

2. In and of themselves, policies do not necessarily solve problems or resolve issues.

3. Temporary policies are not intended as long-term solutions to ingrained problems, nor should they be viewed as such. Such policies need regular review so as not to become, however inadvertently, accepted as permanent institutional policy.

4. Leaders need to be mindful not only of policy formulation, but policy implementation.

5. Stasis and a lack of turnover are not necessarily boons to an institution, particularly when the status quo is far from perfect.

Discussion Questions

1. What factors have prevented Blessed Trinity College from implementing its revised faculty evaluation and contract policies?

2. What are the risks and benefits of this lack of implementation for the institution? For the faculty?

3. What should Carol Roberts do regarding the faculty evaluation and contract policies? Why?

Recommended Background Readings

Benjamin, Ernst. (February 1998). "Five Misconceptions about Tenure." *Trustee-ship*, 3(1): 16–21.

Bess, James L. (1997). *Contract Systems, Bureaucracies, and Faculty Motivation: The Probable Effects of a No-Tenure Policy*. Paper presented at the Annual Meeting of the American Educational Research Association. Chicago, IL, March 1997.

Byrne, J. Peter. (1997). *Academic Freedom Without Tenure?* AAHE New Pathways Working Paper Series, Inquiry #5. Washington, DC: American Association for Higher Education.

Chait, Richard, and Cathy A. Trower. (1997). *Where Tenure Does Not Reign: Colleges with Contract Systems*. AAHE Working Paper Series, Inquiry #3. Washington, DC: American Association for Higher Education.

Gappa, Judith M. (1996). *Off the Tenure Track: Six Models for Full-time Non-tenurable Appointments*. New Pathways Working Paper Series, Inquiry #10. Washington, DC: American Association for Higher Education.

Licata, Christine M. (June 1998). "Post-Tenure Review: At the Crossroads of Accountability and Opportunity." *AAHE Bulletin*, 3–6.

Mallon, William T. (2000). "Standard Deviations: Faculty Appointment Policies at Institutions Without Tenure." In C. Trower, ed., *Policies on Faculty Appointment: Standard Practices and Unusual Arrangements*. Bolton, MA: Anker.

Miller, Richard I. (1987). *Evaluating Faculty for Promotion and Tenure*. San Francisco: Jossey-Bass.

2

Teaching Note:
Georgia State University
Tackling Salary Inequity, Post-Tenure Review, and Part-Time Employment

The Georgia State University (GSU) case can provide important insights into how innovations in faculty employment and worklife can be developed and implemented. The case examines an integrated set of policy changes regarding faculty salaries, faculty workload, and post-tenure review at a public university. In addition, the case also describes an initiative to convert part-time faculty positions to full-time positions.

This teaching note is designed to support the instructor using this case. The questions, discussion points, and exercises provided here represent a possible approach to teaching the GSU case. As the instructor gains familiarity with this particular case, he or she will likely adapt the outline according to audience and experience.

Goals

This note is based on the following instructional goals for teaching the GSU case:

- To examine how innovative approaches to faculty employment are developed and implemented

This teaching note was prepared for the Project on Faculty Appointments by James P. Honan and Cheryl Sternman Rule and funded by the Pew Charitable Trusts. © 2000 by the President and Fellows of Harvard College.

- To assess alternative approaches to the terms and conditions of faculty employment in areas such as salaries, workload, and post-tenure review

- To analyze emerging approaches regarding the employment of part-time faculty

- To examine how academic leaders can best encourage and facilitate changes in faculty worklife policies

Teaching Plan

The Georgia State University case highlights the challenge and complexity of modifying faculty employment and worklife policies. A list of recommended background readings on issues such as faculty workload, merit pay, post-tenure review, and part-time faculty is included at the end of this teaching note. These readings can be used to supplement and support the instructor's teaching plan for the GSU case. Suggested discussion questions to guide participant preparation are also included at the end of this teaching note.

> *Teaching Tip:* The Georgia State University case presents a detailed description of a number of changes in faculty worklife policies that appear to enjoy some initial success. As such, the case does not present a particularly problematic political or administrative dilemma for discussion participants but, rather, describes an emerging set of policy innovations that are in the early stages of implementation. As a result, the instructor should encourage participants to assess and evaluate the various policy changes in their present form and to consider what risks and benefits the policies may present in the future.

Discussion

The instructor should plan to organize participant discussion of the Georgia State University case around the following themes:

1. Putting faculty employment policies "into play"—identifying inequities and inconsistencies

2. Assessing innovative approaches to faculty worklife

3. The leader's role in fostering and sustaining innovation

It is helpful to begin the conversation by discussing how the Arts and Sciences' leadership team knew there was a problem to begin with. Policy changes sometimes follow a watershed event, crisis, or heated demands for change from disenfranchised constituencies, yet this clearly was not the case at Georgia State. The initial discussion will allow students to reflect on the evolution of the new policies.

Putting Faculty Employment Policies "Into Play"—
Identifying Inequities and Inconsistencies

This opening segment can focus on how the need for new faculty employment policies actually reached the institutional agenda at GSU. The instructor can begin the discussion by posing a question about the powerful role of anecdotes and the need for firm data to measure the fairness and impact of existing, yet often unwritten, policies.

- What signs led Dean Abdelal and others to conclude that the status quo regarding salaries, workload, and evaluation was no longer acceptable?

- How did they go about confirming their suspicions? What type of analysis did they employ?

- Was Dean Abdelal's approach to the part-time faculty's concerns consistent with his approach to other employment issues? If not, in what way was it different?

Discussion leaders can pose a number of subquestions such as: How common do you think it is for faculty employment policies to exist in practice but not in writing? Is tinkering with such practices in the absence of clamor and complaints wise? How risky do you think Dean Abdelal's actions were when he opened up this "can of worms?" What do you imagine the responses were from those faculty members who had received larger salaries, enjoyed lighter workloads, and who did not have to worry about post-tenure evaluations before the new employment policies took effect?

Activity: Ask participants to consider whether issues such as salary inequity and workload incomparability among faculty are common realities at colleges and universities more broadly. They can then discuss what other unwritten "policies" are generally accepted on campuses. Do participants feel all details of faculty worklife and employment should be codified? Or, rather, should some be left open to individual negotiation and be tailored to personal circumstance? How should one identify which policies and practices should remain untouched altogether?

Teaching Tip: Dean Abdelal's policy changes are generally considered quite positive and uncontroversial. The larger point of the potentially controversial nature of tinkering with faculty employment policies should not, however, be omitted from the discussion. The instructor may want to pose a hypothetical question, such as "What if Dean Abdelal had suggested not only merit pay for high performers, but salary decreases for poor performers, as part of the same initiative?" How would participants view his actions then?

Assessing Innovative Approaches to Faculty Worklife

The instructor should engage participants in a review and assessment of the new faculty worklife policies at GSU in this segment of the case discussion. Among the questions that might be posed are:

- Assess the strengths and weaknesses of GSU's new policies regarding salaries, workload, and post-tenure review. Do these policies adequately address some of the problems and disparities Dean Abdelal identified earlier in the case?

- Will the implementation of the new salary, workload, and post-tenure review policies result in a good outcome for GSU? For the faculty? Why or why not?

- Was the conversion of part-time faculty positions to full-time positions a good idea? Why or why not? What are the risks and benefits of doing this?

Common Responses to Questions: Participants may feel that the salary and workload policies create equity and consistency where none existed before. They may have mixed feelings about the public nature of salaries and about being assigned workload credit "numbers" based on work that may, by its very nature, be difficult to quantify. It may be useful for the instructor to explore both the positive and negative aspects of these responses.

Activity: Ask participants to imagine themselves as part-time faculty members at GSU. The instructor can pose the following questions to spur further discussion: How do you feel about your new status and new salary? Do you feel that the administration has listened to, and appropriately responded to, your concerns? If yes, how so? If not, what recourse do you have now that discussion of this issue has, for the time being at least, subsided? Do any concerns remain?

The Leader's Role in Fostering and Sustaining Innovation

This segment of the discussion focuses on Dean Abdelal's style and effectiveness as a leader and as a change agent. The following questions aim to elicit discussion of Abdelal's approach and how his leadership style affected not only the development, but the ultimate effectiveness and acceptance, of his policy revisions:

- Assess the strengths and weaknesses of Dean Abdelal's leadership style and strategies in this case. Are there things you think he should have done differently? Why?

- Do the innovations developed by Dean Abdelal and his colleagues at GSU appear to be sustainable? What accounts for this? Are there particular "success factors" that have contributed to this outcome?

- What should academic leaders do to support and encourage innovations in faculty worklife? Are there pitfalls they should avoid? Which?

Activity: Engage participants in a brief exercise to identify the characteristics of an innovative academic leader. Possible questions include: Are there some faculty employment issues around which it is more acceptable, or safer, to innovate than others? Must an academic leader enjoy widespread popularity in order to lead an effective change process? Does an innovative policy necessarily mean a better policy?

The instructor may distribute the case update at the end of this note toward the end of the discussion. This update provides additional information on the status of the various policy reforms at GSU. As a way of generating discussion of the update, the instructor can pose questions such as: Does the information provided in the case update raise any concerns for you with regard to the results of the initial implementation of the revised policies? Does the information provided in the case update constitute "forward progress" for Dean Abdelal and his colleagues at GSU?

Wrap-Up: Learning Points and Take-Aways

The instructor's concluding remarks and review of points raised during the discussion of the GSU case can include the following lessons and insights.

1. It can be helpful to take a holistic view of faculty employment policies to ensure that each policy element supports the goals of related policy elements. The GSU case highlights the important links among salaries, workload, and post-tenure review.

2. The availability of resources (financial and human) plays an essential role in the successful modification of faculty employment policies and in the conversion of part-time positions.

3. The leader's style and approach in fostering and sustaining innovation is a significant success factor in reviewing and revising faculty worklife policies and practices.

Discussion Questions

1. What are the strengths and weaknesses of Dean Abdelal's integrated strategy regarding faculty salaries, workload, and evaluation policies for ranked faculty at GSU?

2. What is your assessment of GSU's conversion of part-time instructors to full-time, non-tenure-track positions? Is this effort good for the institution? For the faculty? Why or why not?

3. What challenges and dilemmas might face GSU regarding faculty employment and worklife in the future? How should Dean Abdelal and his colleagues address them if they arise?

Recommended Background Readings

Abdelal, Ahmed T. et al. (1997). "Integrating Accountability Systems and Reward Structures: Workload Policy, Post-Tenure Evaluations, and Salary Compensation." *Metropolitan Universities*, 7(4): 61–73.

Diamond, Robert M., and Bronwyn E. Adam, eds. (1993). *Recognizing Faculty Work: Reward Systems for the Year 2000*. San Francisco: Jossey-Bass.

Gappa, Judith M., and David W. Leslie, eds. (1993). *The Invisible Faculty: Improving the Status of Part-Timers in Higher Education*. San Francisco: Jossey-Bass.

Gappa, Judith M., and David W. Leslie. (1997). *Two Faculties or One? The Conundrum of Part-Timers in a Bifurcated Workforce*. New Pathways Working Paper Series, Inquiry #6. Washington, DC: American Association for Higher Education.

Hansen, W. L. (1988). "Merit Pay in Higher Education." In David W. Breneman and Ted I. K. Youn, eds., *Academic Labor Markets and Careers* (114–137). New York: Falmer Press.

Layzell, Daniel T. (1999). "Higher Education's Changing Environment: Faculty Productivity and the Reward Structure." In William G. Tierney, ed., *Faculty Productivity: Facts, Fictions, and Issues*. New York: Falmer Press.

Licata, Christine M., and Joseph C. Morreale. (1997). *Post-Tenure Review: Policies, Practices, Precautions*. New Pathways Working Paper Series, Inquiry #12. Washington, DC: American Association for Higher Education.

Reichard, Gary W. (1998). "Part-Time Faculty in Research Universities: Problems and Prospects." *Academe*, 84 (January/February): 4–43.

Rhoades, Gary. (1996). "Reorganizing the Faculty Workforce for Flexibility." *Journal of Higher Education*, 67(6): 626–659.

Case Update: Georgia State University

On May 12, 2000, Dean Abdelal provided the following update on the recent changes in the College of Arts and Sciences.

> *Significant progress in conversion is occurring.* Last year we were successful in securing the necessary resources to replace part-time instructor (PTI) positions with full-time, one-year visiting positions. Currently, the only PTI sections in our college are taught by profes-

sionals who are employed full-time in their respective disciplines in the greater Atlanta area. This year we have secured additional resources to establish twenty-five new tenure-track positions and twenty-five new regular non-tenure-track lecturer positions. A number of searches throughout the college have been completed while a number are still in progress. Visiting and temporary faculty were invited to apply for these positions. Departmental faculty committees conducted all the searches in accordance with the hiring policies of Georgia State University. Some of the visiting faculty members were successful candidates for either tenure-track or regular non-tenure-track positions while others were not. The regular lecturer positions are continuing appointments that are subject to renewal with notification following the same timeline that applies to tenure-track appointments. The function of successful candidates for these positions is primarily teaching and service, with limited expectations in scholarly activity. The policy of the board of regents specifies that these appointments should be renewed beyond the sixth year only if the candidate is deemed to be outstanding in instruction (see www.peachnet.edu/admin/humex/policy/sec800.html; Section 803.03). The dean's office's interpretation of the policies governing such appointments is that once performance has been assessed as outstanding, the only likely circumstance that could result in nonrenewal is an unexpected significant drop in student demand in the relevant department. Thus, we believe that these positions carry considerable job security beyond the sixth year of employment for those lecturers who demonstrate excellence in instruction.

Decisions about staffing configurations are undertaken according to specified criteria. As part of the planning process for Academic Year 2001, the dean's office asked each department to project the number of visiting positions and regular non-tenure-track lecturer positions needed, based on their assessment of curricular needs and the number of tenure-track faculty positions that they were authorized to fill. The dean's office takes several considerations into account in making decisions with respect to the numbers and types of positions to be funded in a given department. The first of these is the balance between courses in general education (i.e., core curriculum), courses for undergraduate majors, and courses for graduate majors. A department, such as English, with a relatively high percent of required introductory core courses would be expected to meet its obligations through a mix of tenure-track, regular non-tenure-track, and visiting appointments. In contrast, a department with limited offerings and responsibilities in the core curriculum would be expected to have far fewer non-tenure-track positions (regular or visiting). The second consideration is whether the terminal degree in the department is the master's or Ph.D. The curricular needs of doctoral programs argue against having more than a few non-tenure-track positions. The third consideration is the outcome of academic program review. Georgia State University has a formal process that involves a departmental self-study; assessments by outside evaluators and a standing committee of the university senate; and assessments by both the dean's office and the provost's office. The review process culminates in an action plan that might commit the university to a specific course of action and specific funding.

One can achieve a better understanding of our model and future goals by focusing on staffing in departments that have substantial responsibilities in general education (e.g., English, mathematics, or modern languages). In general, our long-term goal in these departments is to limit the use of visiting faculty to less than 10 percent of the total faculty of the department. We plan to implement this goal through incremental replacement of visiting positions with regular tenure-track and non-tenure-track positions. However, an additional layer of complexity arises because of the inability at this time to make reasonable estimates of student need for various core courses at Georgia State University. This inability to project student demand derives in part from our being in the midst of a major change in the undergraduate student body, a change that is propelled in one direction by demographics, the availability of HOPE scholarships, and residential housing and is propelled in the opposite direction by the incremental implementation of higher freshman admission requirements that were mandated by the board of regents. A second challenge in making reasonable projections of student demand is the absence of long-term data regarding the likely student choices among alternatives in a core curriculum that was implemented at the time of conversion from the quarter calendar to the semester calendar in fall 1998. I expect that these factors will preclude accurate projections for two or three additional years.

It follows from the preceding analysis that while we plan to add new tenure-track and regular non-tenure-track positions in departments with major responsibilities in the core curriculum, the specific numbers of these two types of positions as well as the number of visiting positions needed will have to be determined annually for the next several years. As we have emphasized from the beginning of the conversion from the PTI model, filling the available visiting positions in any department will be carried out through searches that will be advertised in the university and in the Atlanta newspapers whereas filling regular tenure-track and non-tenure-track positions will be carried out through searches that will be advertised in appropriate national professional outlets. In all cases, the searches will obviously adhere to the normal search procedures of the university. In the meantime, we plan to increase compensation for visiting instructors and visiting lecturers from $24,000 and $30,000, respectively, to $26,000 and $32,000 for next year.

3

Teaching Note:
Kansas State University
Evaluating and Addressing
Chronic Low Achievement

The Kansas State University (K-State) case study examines a series of events that, in response to a regents' mandate, led to the development of new faculty evaluation policies. The policies were intended to identify chronic low performers among K-State's tenured faculty and to define remediation procedures for performance-related problems and concerns. The case also addresses questions concerning shared governance and organizational change, focusing on the roles of regents, senior administrators, department chairs, and faculty in academic policy development and decision making.

This teaching note is designed to support the instructor using this case. The questions, discussion points, and exercises provided have proven effective in prior teaching of this case with a wide range of participant groups. As the instructor gains familiarity with this particular case, he or she will likely adapt the outline according to audience and experience.

Goals

This note is based on the following instructional goals for teaching the K-State case:

This teaching note was prepared for the Project on Faculty Appointments by James P. Honan, Susan B. Kenyon, and Cheryl Sternman Rule and funded by the Pew Charitable Trusts. © 2000 by the President and Fellows of Harvard College.

- To examine factors that trigger campus discussions and policy deliberations concerning faculty evaluation

- To analyze the processes through which faculty evaluation policies are discussed, deliberated, and developed

- To identify ways to assess the effectiveness and outcomes of faculty evaluation procedures

- To identify data elements that would assist in this assessment

Teaching Plan

Begin the session by exploring the growing interest in evaluating and assessing college and university faculty and, in particular, the growing interest in evaluating the work of tenured faculty. The work of Christine Licata and others (see Recommended Background Readings) can be referenced and described (frameworks for thinking about post-tenure review, range of policy examples and models, and comparative data on specific evaluation policies and procedures) as a way of putting the K-State case study into a broader national context. National data and statistics on the evaluation of tenured faculty might also be presented. Suggested discussion questions to guide participant preparation are also included at the end of this teaching note.

Discussion

Plan to organize participant discussion of the K-State case around the following themes:

1. Problem identification, policy objectives, and policy context
2. Analysis of K-State faculty evaluation policies
3. Assessment of policy outcomes and data needs for assessment

Problem Identification, Policy Objectives, and Policy Context

This first theme, a three-part general entry into the case, should be broken down such that each individual element is treated separately.

Problem Identification. The instructor may wish to begin the case discussion by asking a broad question directed at problem identification, or analysis of the policy objectives and policy context of the K-State case. Sample opening questions include:

- Who is trying to solve what problem in this case?

- Why is a conversation about faculty evaluation policies taking place on the K-State campus?

- With regard to the regents' mandate, why aren't the regents concerned about identifying and rewarding high achievers rather than focusing on chronic low performers?

- Should chronic low performers on campus, faculty and administrators, be identified internally?

Subquestions might focus on the particular interests and goals of various constituents in the case: regents, provost, president, chairs, and faculty.

Activity: If the instructor so chooses, a discussion-facilitating exercise may be used at this point. Divide participants into three role-play groups: regents, provost, and faculty. Organize the role play discussion as follows:

Regents group: What do you hope to accomplish with this mandate? What are your policy objectives?

Provost group: In light of the regents' mandate, what do you hope to achieve?

Faculty group: What do you do now that this issue is on your plate? Is the regents' request reasonable? Should the faculty resist?

An overarching question that can be posed to all three groups is: What pitfalls must you work to avoid?

Policy Objectives. This second major segment of the case discussion should highlight aspects of the case that deal with shared governance and organizational change issues. Examples of questions that might engage participants in a discussion of these issues include:

- Was the provost wise to delegate the issue to the faculty senate immediately?

- Was there a realistic alternative?

- Did this move represent an effective strategy for organizational change? Why or why not?

Teaching Tip: If it does not come up in the discussion, it is worth noting to discussion participants that K-State's president and provost had invested significant political capital over the years in shared governance mechanisms, and now some of that "banked capital" has to be withdrawn. It is also important to note that there was stable leadership at K-State and that both senior administrators and various faculty and governance groups were fairly familiar with one another based on previous discussions regarding faculty evaluation and related issues. Such policy discussions would be significantly more difficult to convene in the early years of a provost's or president's tenure.

Policy Context. This part of the case discussion should focus on the policy context within which the deliberation of C31.5 and related faculty evaluation policies was taking place. Good questions to include here are:

- What is your assessment of the context within which discussions of faculty evaluation policies at K-State were taking place?

- Was it a good time for such discussions to be taking place? Why or why not?

- To what extent was the campus prepared or not prepared for such policy deliberations?

- What is your assessment of the way in which the provost and others approached the policy discussions?

- Are there any alternative strategies that you would have employed in this situation?

Analysis of K-State's Faculty Evaluation Policies

This second major segment of the case discussion should focus specifically on the faculty evaluation policies developed at K-State: C31.5, C31.6, C31.7, and C.31.8 (refer participants to relevant pages in the case for specific references to policy statements). Opening questions for the analysis could be:

- Do these policies meet the objectives that were discussed earlier? Why or why not?

- Under K-State's newly established faculty evaluation policies, could we discover, if we wanted to, who the chronic low performing faculty are?

- If so, should we?

- If we do this, who should know the names of chronic low performers?

Teaching Tip: It is possible that some participants will note that the new faculty evaluation policies are very complex and that it is difficult to fully address the question about whether they do or do not meet stated policy objectives. Aside from the technical feasibility of being able to identify chronic low performers, participants should also explore what is politically feasible in this situation. It is helpful to acknowledge these considerations, then to explore the complexities of the policies in more detail.

Once participants have exhausted the overarching questions regarding stated policy objectives, direct the discussion to more specific aspects of the policies including:

- The balance or tension between department- or unit-based implementation of the policies versus university-wide implementation (a distributed versus centralized approach to faculty evaluation)

- Minimum departmental standards for faculty productivity versus individual, faculty specific goals

- Resource allocation (assignment of responsibilities and allocation of time) implications of policies versus impact on productivity of individual faculty

- Overall performance of faculty versus specific elements of performance critical to the mission of the department

Questions to pose concerning these complexities include:

- How important is each aspect of the policy to your overall assessment of K-State's faculty evaluation policies?

- Would you shift the emphasis of K-State's policy to the opposite side of the continuum in any of the above pairings? Why or why not?

- What would such shifts enable the institution to accomplish?

It might also be useful to pose more specific subquestions regarding the following topics: "overall performance," resource allocation, and differences in departmental approaches to evaluation standards. In reference to "overall performance," questions that might be asked include: Why is this issue so crucial? Should the provost "go to the mat" on the issue? Questions that might be posed concerning resource allocation include:

- How does the concept of "overall performance" relate to the provost's concern about resource allocation?

- If a faculty member does not prove to be effective in the classroom, is it fair and sensible to assign that individual more research time?

- Conversely, should the most productive teachers be freed from the classroom? Isn't that just what concerns the public and the regents?

It can also be worthwhile to highlight some of the differences in approach (qualitative versus quantitative, stringent versus lax, specific versus flexible) that the various academic departments have undertaken to implement the new evaluation policies. Refer participants to Table 3.1 (Minimum Performance Standards) in the case. A discussion of the pros and cons of the various approaches can be conducted during this segment.

Another area of discussion in this segment might focus on the role department chairs play in the implementation of the new faculty evaluation policies and with regard to the initiation of the remediation process for faculty who are identified as chronic low performers. Possible questions to pose might include:

- In what ways have the new faculty evaluation policies changed the department chairs' role at K-State?

- What role do department chairs play regarding the success or failure of implementing the new faculty evaluation procedures?

- What special challenges arise for department chairs as K-State implements its new evaluation policies? Possible topics for discussion here include: the changing relationship and role of K-State's department chairs to faculty colleagues under the new policies and the potential impact of rotating or revolving department chairs.

Assessment of Policy Outcomes and Data Needs for Assessment

The final segment of the case discussion should focus on the extent to which participants in the case discussion believe that the K-State faculty evaluation policies represent a positive outcome. This conversation might be convened from the perspectives of various constituents in the case: regents, provost, president, deans, chairs, and faculty and can focus on the question: What has been accomplished according to whose perspective? Possible questions to open this portion of the discussion include:

- What has been accomplished so far at K-State regarding faculty evaluation?

- Do these accomplishments represent a positive outcome for K-State? Why or why not?

- What remaining or lingering concerns do you have concerning the outcome at the end of the case?

As the instructor begins to wrap up the discussion, questions should focus on the future impact of K-State's faculty evaluation policies.

- What will change in practice?

- What will be the most noticeable impact of these policies five years from now? Probe for specific examples.

A good follow-up question would be:

- What kinds of data would you want to collect on an ongoing basis to measure the impact of the new faculty evaluation policies at K-State?

Common responses to this question include: financial costs of implementing the new evaluation policies; trends regarding the number of faculty identified as chronic low performers; trends regarding the number of complaints about faculty from students or parents to legislators and regents; instances of intrusion by regents in the future on faculty promotion and tenure decisions; analyses of improved learning outcomes among students; and examples of successful remediation.

An effective closing question for this line of conversation is: Should these data be made public? Why or why not?

Teaching Tip: The instructor may also want to initiate a more generalized summary discussion focused on comparing and contrasting K-State's faculty evaluation policies with more universal post-tenure review policies (perhaps using Licata's framework). The discussion might focus on putting K-State's faculty evaluation policies into a national context and comparing the university's efforts with those undertaken by other colleges and universities focusing on both the policies themselves and on the impetus for developing the policies in the first place (regents' mandate, legislative requirements, faculty-generated policies, and so on). National comparative data on faculty employment policies and procedures is available from the Project on Faculty Appointments' Faculty Appointment Policy Archive (FAPA), a CD-ROM tool that would assist K-State case discussion participants in class discussions and in support of preparing class assignments or papers on comparative analyses of such policies.

Wrap-Up: Learning Points and Take-Aways

As a way of wrapping up the K-State case discussion, some pertinent learning points and take-aways include:

1. It is important to be aware of the impetus for policy discussions of faculty employment issues. In this case, the regents' mandate for revising faculty development policies triggered the events in the case, and meeting the requirements of this mandate was reflected in the policies that were ultimately created. Policy discussions at other institutions might be convened in response to other triggers (such as legislatures, presidents, or provosts) and result in alternative outcomes; it is important to understand such differences.

2. Leadership style, governance issues, and process are important ingredients for effective policy deliberations concerning faculty employment policies. In this case, the fact that there was stable leadership at the institution and that there had been prior campus conversations concerning faculty evaluation policies through existing governance structures made it possible for sustained policy deliberations to take place and for subsequent policy implementation. These factors are important to the overall understanding of reviewing and revising faculty employment policies.

3. Processes for reviewing and revising faculty employment policies should include some discussion of desired outcomes and means for assessing improved policies and procedures. Questions such as, "What are we trying to accomplish through modifications in policy?" and "How will we know if we have accomplished our goals?" are worth raising while policies are being reviewed and modified.

Discussion Questions

1. Does the passage of Sections C31.5, C31.6, C31.7, and C31.8 adequately address the board of regents' concern about faculty performance and accountability? Why or why not?

2. Does the fact that Sections C31.5–C31.8 are implemented primarily on a departmental level make it more or less likely that potential faculty productivity problems will be identified and corrected?

3. Did the passage and implementation of Sections C31.5–C31.8 result in a good outcome at K-State? Why or why not?

4. What is your overall assessment of K-State's approach to organizational change? What elements of their change strategy are most significant to you? Why?

Recommended Background Readings

Centra, John A. (1993). *Reflective Faculty Evaluation: Enhancing Teaching and Determining Faculty Effectiveness.* San Francisco: Jossey-Bass.

Chait, Richard P. (1998). "Post-Tenure Review of Department." In *Ideas in Incubation: Three Possible Modifications to Traditional Tenure Policies.* Washington, DC: American Association for Higher Education, pp. 13–20.

Goodman, Madeleine J. (1994). "The Review of Tenured Faculty at a Research University: Outcomes and Appraisals." *The Review of Higher Education* 18(1): 83–94.

Licata, Christine M., and Joseph C. Morreale, (1997). *Post-Tenure Review: Policies, Practices, Precautions.* New Pathways Working Paper Series, Inquiry #12, Washington, DC: American Association for Higher Education.

Project on Faculty Appointments. (1999). "Faculty Appointment Policy Archive" (CD-ROM). Cambridge, MA: Harvard Graduate School of Education.

Seldin, Peter (1990). *How Administrators Can Improve Teaching: Moving From Talk to Action in Higher Education.* San Francisco: Jossey-Bass.

4

Teaching Note:
Olivet College
Aligning Faculty Employment
Policies with an Evolving Mission

The Olivet College case study focuses on a small, private college's experiences with changes in faculty tenure policies. The case details these changes over a twenty-five year period, examining a move away from traditional tenure in the early 1970s followed by a possible reconsideration of this move in the mid- to late-1990s. The Olivet case can serve as an excellent tool for discussing the pros and cons of traditional tenure policies, the challenges of implementing policy changes regarding the terms and conditions of faculty employment, and the dilemmas institutions of higher education face as they attempt to align faculty employment policies and faculty roles and responsibilities with institutional mission and strategic plans.

This teaching note is designed to support the instructor using this case. The questions, discussion points, and exercises provided here represent one possible approach to teaching the Olivet College case. As the instructor gains familiarity with the Olivet case, he or she will likely adapt the outline according to audience and experience.

This teaching note was prepared for the Project on Faculty Appointments by James P. Honan and Susan B. Kenyon and funded by the Pew Charitable Trusts. © 2000 by the President and Fellows of Harvard College.

Goals

The teaching note is based on the following instructional goals for teaching the Olivet College case:

- To explore the advantages and disadvantages of traditional tenure policies

- To examine institutional change processes regarding faculty employment policies and the terms and conditions of faculty employment

- To analyze the connections between faculty employment policies and institutional mission and strategic plans

- To assess the implications of modifying faculty roles and responsibilities in relation to the roles and responsibilities of administrators and staff

Teaching Plan

The Olivet College case provides the instructor and class participants with the opportunity to engage in a discussion of the complex and challenging process of changing an institution's approach to one of the most fundamental features of faculty employment—

Teaching Tip: The Olivet College case can serve as an effective tool for engaging faculty and staff in a productive conversation of the fundamental role they each play in the teaching and learning process. It is important to note the unique characteristics of a small, private institution such as Olivet at the beginning of the case discussion and to acknowledge the different perspectives that faculty and staff will bring to the case discussion. In addition, it can be helpful to encourage discussion participants to consider the extent to which the policy changes made at Olivet would or would not make sense in their own institutional settings.

tenure. Suggested discussion questions to guide participant preparation are included at the end of this teaching note.

Opening remarks from the instructor regarding the relevance of this case to the current policy environment could focus on the current status and prevalence of tenure policies among colleges and universities (see Recommended Background Readings at the end of this teaching note) and on some of the key policy questions and debates regarding faculty tenure. It is important to note that most institutions have some form of tenure policy and that Olivet's experiences are somewhat unique. A relatively small number of institutions have moved from having tenure to not having tenure or from not having tenure to having tenure. It is also important to note up front that most of the institutions that have considered and implemented such policy changes are small, private institutions.

Discussion

The instructor should plan to organize participant discussion of the Olivet College case around the following themes:

1. Analysis of Olivet faculty employment policies: policy objectives
2. Linking employment policies with mission and strategic plans: policy context
3. Faculty employment policies and institutional transformation

Analysis of Olivet Faculty Employment Policies: Policy Objectives

The initial segment of the discussion of the Olivet College case should consist of a description and analysis of Olivet's faculty employment policies and policy objectives throughout the time period covered by the case.

As described in the case text, Olivet's faculty employment policies during the past twenty-five years have included a traditional tenure system (pre-1974) and a five-year contract system (instituted in 1973–74 and utilized as of 2000). A return to a traditional tenure system was proposed by President Michael Bassis in fall 1994 but had not been implemented as of 2000. This section of the case discussion should focus on these three iterations of faculty employment policies and the related policy objectives of each. Questions to be posed regarding each policy (pre-1974 tenure system, 1973–2000 five-year contract system, and 1994 proposed tenure policy) include:

- What are the important elements and key objectives of Olivet's three iterations of faculty employment policies?

- What iteration of Olivet's faculty employment policy is most advantageous to the faculty? Why?

- What version of Olivet's faculty employment is best for the institution? Why?

The instructor can pose a number of subquestions to deepen the discussion generated by the above questions. For example, the discussion of key elements of the three policy approaches can be further advanced by posing a question such as: How does each policy work in practice for an individual Olivet faculty member? Questions regarding policy objectives can follow, such as: What is the college trying to accomplish by implementing this policy? What broader goals is the college hoping to achieve? Finally, additional questions about the advantages and disadvantages of each policy approach for the faculty and for the institution can be posed to generate a more generic conversation about the pros and cons of faculty tenure policies.

Common Responses to Questions. It is possible that the initial segment of the Olivet case discussion might focus quite specifically on the pros and cons of tenure. If and when this occurs, the instructor might encourage participants to distinguish between an analytic approach to the issue of tenure and an ideological or subjective perspective on the subject. Depending on the audience for the case discussion, the instructor may have to underscore this distinction. For example, if the discussion participants consist primarily of faculty, then the instructor may need to assume a "devil's advocate" position by asking participants to identify and discuss the disadvantages of tenure. Ideally, this portion of the discussion should generate multiple perspectives concerning the advantages and disadvantages of various approaches to faculty employment policy.

Activity: Engage the discussion participants in a brief exercise concerning the advantages and disadvantages of each of the three iterations of the faculty employment policies as viewed from the perspective of an Olivet faculty member. Ask participants to imagine themselves as an Olivet faculty member and to address the following questions: What iteration of the faculty employment policies is most appealing to you? Why? What concerns does each version of the college's faculty employment policies raise for you? A variation of this exercise might involve asking the participants to imagine themselves as a candidate for a faculty position at Olivet and inviting participants to consider the following questions: Under which version of Olivet's policy would you most like to work? Why? Still another variation on this exercise could highlight the administrative perspective by asking participants to consider the following questions: If you were an administrator at Olivet, what version of the faculty employment policies would be most appealing to you? Why? What concerns do you have about each version of the college's faculty employment policies?

Teaching Tip: Since this segment of the case discussion describes Olivet's three iterations of its faculty employment policies and related policy objectives, it may be helpful to create a three-column matrix with the headings "Pre-1974 Tenure Policy," "1973-74–2000 Five-year Contract System," and "1994 Proposed Tenure Policy." The instructor can then ask participants to describe the key elements of each policy and to identify the primary policy objectives which each policy seeks to achieve. The matrix will provide important information which can be referenced in the next segment of the case discussion.

Linking Employment Policies with Mission
and Strategic Plans: Policy Context

This segment of the discussion should focus on the institutional context within which Olivet is contemplating changes in its faculty employment policies and other campus processes. Two questions to initiate this particular discussion are: What are the key elements of Olivet's new vision statement (Education for Individual and Social Responsibility) and the Olivet Plan? What are the implications of these documents for faculty roles and responsibilities at the college?

Other questions include:

- What are the implications of the "everyone is an educator" concept for faculty at Olivet?

- What are the ultimate goals and purposes of Olivet's new vision statement and the Olivet Plan? To what extent are the college's faculty employment policies and procedures aligned with these goals and purposes?

The instructor can deepen the conversation about the relationship between Olivet's vision statement and plan and the terms and conditions of faculty employment by posing questions about the possible inconsistencies between the college's aspirations and current patterns of faculty and staff roles. For example, the instructor might try to push the "everyone is an educator" concept to its limit and ask: Should faculty, administrators, and staff at Olivet play exactly the same roles in the teaching and learning process? Should the terms and conditions of employment (length of contract, salary levels, evaluation criteria, workload, and so on) be identical for faculty and staff? Do faculty and staff at Olivet enjoy the same sense of power and influence in the college's overall governance structure? These types of questions will enable discussion participants to truly grapple with the challenges of redefining faculty and staff roles and responsibilities as well as highlight the difficulties inherent in the development of common employment, appointment, and evaluation policies for each group.

Common Responses to Questions. Responses to the above questions may raise additional issues such as: Who is an educator in a college or university setting and how can an institution best establish policies that recognize and support the contributions and development of all employees? What are the limits of removing boundaries among faculty and staff roles and responsibilities? What impact might this nontraditional approach to defining faculty and administrative roles have on the quality and demographic profile of the applicant pool for faculty positions?

Activity: Divide the class up into two groups: faculty and administrators (or staff). Ask each group to address the following issue: The new vision statement (Education for Individual and Social Responsibility) and the Olivet Plan both contain ideas and principles that suggest that faculty and administrators or staff will need to rethink their respective roles and responsibilities and revisit core assumptions about power and decision making. As a faculty member (one group) or as an administrator or staff member (the other group) at Olivet, what modifications will need to be made regarding your roles and responsibilities in order to implement the core ideas of the vision statement and plan? After giving the groups some time to deliberate (fifteen to twenty minutes), the instructor can then record the key ideas generated and invite participants to compare and contrast each group's suggestions and the implications of these suggestions for faculty roles and responsibilities at Olivet. The instructor might also ask participants to consider the internal and external dimensions of the various modifications to faculty and administrative roles and responsibilities.

Teaching Tip: It is important to fully explore the implications of Olivet's vision statement and plan for the roles that faculty and administrators or staff play at the college. The instructor should explicitly press class participants to think about the "everyone is an educator" concept as it relates to employment policies, roles and responsibilities, criteria for evaluation of faculty and administrators or staff, and governance structures and policies. To put this segment of the discussion in a broader context, it may be useful to identify pertinent reading and institutional examples from other colleges and universities. If particular participants are actually faculty members, administrators, or staff members, it is helpful to remind them to think beyond the roles they currently play so that they can fully engage in the case discussion of the respective roles and responsibilities of both groups.

Faculty Employment Policies and Institutional Transformation

The final segment of the Olivet case discussion links the two prior segments dealing with faculty employment policies and the policy context at Olivet with the college's broader efforts regarding institutional transformation. Possible questions to generate discussion of these issues include:

- Should Olivet adopt a traditional tenure policy for faculty? Why or why not?

- What is your interpretation of the Olivet faculty's apparent reluctance to support a return to traditional tenure?

- Can the work of the Olivet Employee Plan Project Group help to inform a decision regarding a possible return to traditional tenure? How?

- What role should newly appointed President F. J. Talley play in the deliberations concerning tenure policy and institutional transformation? Are there any particular strategies that might be effective?

- What would be a good outcome for Olivet College regarding tenure policy?

- What would be a good outcome for Olivet's overall transformation aspirations?

Common Responses to Questions. Since it is likely that the discussion of these questions will focus on the pros and cons of moving away from or returning to a traditional tenure policy, it is helpful for the instructor to provide a brief context for this type of policy reform. (See Mallon [2002] in Recommended Background Readings at the end of this teaching note for examples of institutions moving toward or away from tenure.) In addition, it is important to ask participants to grapple with the pros and cons of moving away from or toward tenure without adopting a simplistic interpretation such as thinking moving away from tenure is necessarily negative and moving toward tenure is necessarily positive. The Olivet case provides participants with an opportunity to consider these policy reforms in a more complex manner since the institution has had experience with both alternatives.

Activity: Engage participants in a brief exercise concerning tenure policy and institutional transformation. Ask participants to consider the extent to which the proposed return to tenure might help or hinder the college's overall transformation agenda. Participants could be divided into small groups and asked to assume the role of various constituents (trustee, president, provost, faculty member, staff member, administrator, student). Groups might address the following questions for a brief period of time (ten to fifteen minutes): Would a return to traditional tenure be a good thing from your perspective? Would a return to traditional tenure help or hinder Olivet's efforts to transform itself? Following these deliberations, the instructor could then ask each group to report on the highlights of their respective discussions from the various constituent viewpoints.

Teaching Tip: This segment of the case discussion can serve as a particularly effective forum for a conversation about the fundamental purpose of faculty tenure and its relationship to overall institutional mission, values, and transformation efforts. Focus on such issues as the faculty's apparent lack of support for a return to traditional tenure, the strong support the Olivet community appears to give to the overall institutional transformation initiative, and the potential misalignment of a traditional tenure policy and the "everyone is an educator" concept.

Wrap-Up: Learning Points and Take-Aways

The instructor can conclude the discussion of the Olivet College case by reminding participants that this is a somewhat unique situation that nonetheless raises some fundamental questions about the role that faculty play in the educational process and the ways in which faculty employment policies, governance structures, and evaluation criteria need to be aligned with overall institutional mission, vision, and culture.

Implications, lessons, and insights from the Olivet College case might include:

1. Faculty employment policies are directly linked to and influenced by overall institutional mission, plans, and culture, but it is challenging to craft policies that align mission and plans with faculty and staff roles and responsibilities.

2. Changing faculty employment policies has implications for the overall identity and culture of an organization. A change in faculty employment policies has a direct impact on issues such as recruitment, governance, evaluation, and retention.

3. Faculty employment policies need to be tailored to specific institutional missions and contexts. This case presents an interesting example of a situation where traditional tenure

policies, while a predominant feature of employment policies at colleges and universities throughout the United States, do not appear to be universally adopted as the only approach to establishing the terms and conditions of faculty employment.

Discussion Questions

1. Evaluate Olivet College's three approaches to faculty employment policy. Which one is most effective? Why?

2. In what ways should Olivet College modify its faculty employment policies to align them more closely with the values and concepts inherent in the Olivet Plan and the new vision statement, Education for Individual Social Responsibility?

3. Should Olivet College return to a system of traditional tenure for faculty? Why or why not?

Recommended Background Readings

Austin, Ann E., R. Eugene Rice, Allen P. Splete, and Associates. (1991). A Good Place to Work: Sourcebook for the Academic Workplace. Washington, DC: Council of Independent Colleges.

Breneman, David W. (1997). Alternatives to Tenure for the Next Generation of Academics. New Pathways Working Paper Series, Inquiry #14. Washington, DC: American Association for Higher Education.

Chait, Richard. (1998). Ideas in Incubation: Three Possible Modifications to Traditional Tenure Policies. New Pathways Working Paper Series, Inquiry #9. Washington, DC: American Association for Higher Education.

Chait, Richard, and Cathy A. Trower. (1997). Where Tenure Does Not Reign: Colleges With Contract Systems. New Pathways Working Paper Series, Inquiry #3. Washington, DC: American Association for Higher Education.

Magrath, C. Peter. (1997). "Eliminating Tenure Without Destroying Academic Freedom." Trusteeship, 5(3): 16-19.

Mallon, William T. (2002). "Why Is Tenure One College's Problem and Another's Solution?" In Richard P. Chait, ed., The Questions of Tenure. Cambridge, MA: Harvard University Press.

Mangan, Katherine S. (1989). "Four Colleges' Experiences with Alternatives to Traditional Tenure." *Chronicle of Higher Education*, March 1, p. A10.

Trower, Cathy A. (1996). *Tenure Snapshot*. New Pathways Working Paper Series, Inquiry #2. Washington, DC: American Association for Higher Education.

Yarmolinsky, Adam. (1996). "Tenure: Permanence and Change: A Case for the Flexible Contract." *Change*, 28(3): 16–20.

5

Teaching Note:
University of Central Arkansas
Transformative Leadership, Premium Contracts, and a New Identity

The University of Central Arkansas (UCA) case study examines two attempts at implementing innovative policies and management structures within a public institution of higher education. These two efforts—one focusing on a proposed salary plan designed to pay faculty a sizable salary premium in lieu of entering the tenure track, the other involving the possible transformation of UCA into a "charter university"—provide an ideal platform for robust discussions of presidential leadership, innovative approaches to faculty employment policies, shared governance, organizational change, and unique management and governance structures for public higher education institutions.

This teaching note is designed to support the instructor using this case. The questions, discussion points, and exercises provided here have proven effective in prior teaching of the UCA case. As the instructor gains familiarity with this particular case, he or she should adapt the outline according to audience and experience.

This teaching note was prepared for the Project on Faculty Appointments by James P. Honan, Susan B. Kenyon, and Cheryl Sternman Rule and funded by the Pew Charitable Trusts. © 2000 by the President and Fellows of Harvard College.

Goals

This note is based on the following instructional goals for teaching the University of Central Arkansas case:

- To explore approaches to encouraging innovation and organizational change in public colleges and universities

- To examine policy issues and dilemmas concerning tenure and faculty compensation

- To analyze presidential leadership as a force for promoting organizational change

- To identify and assess alternative management and governance structures for public higher education

Teaching Plan

The University of Central Arkansas case can serve as the basis for discussion of several emerging challenges in the higher education policy environment, including the development and creation of alternative faculty appointments (full-time, non-tenure-track appointments in particular) within an institutional context that includes tenure-track and tenured faculty; the transformation of traditional colleges and universities into charter colleges; and leadership approaches to fostering organizational change and innovation. Recommended readings on these topics can serve as excellent supplements to the UCA case (see Recommended Background Readings at the end of this teaching note). Suggested discussion questions to guide participant preparation are also noted at the end of this teaching note.

> *Teaching Tip:* The University of Central Arkansas case presents a complex and rich account of a number of important leadership and policy issues facing colleges and universities. Depending on the audience and on the instructor's preferences, class discussions of this case can highlight presidential leadership and leadership style, faculty governance issues, innovation and change in higher education, tenure policy and alternative approaches to faculty employment and compensation, and the charter college or university concept.

If the instructor intends to use the case to focus on the creation of alternative faculty appointments, opening remarks could focus on the growth in and widening popularity of non-tenure-track appointments in recent years (see Magner, 2000; O'Neill, 2000). If the intended focal point for the discussion is the development of charter colleges and universities, the instructor might open the discussion by citing and highlighting recent institutional examples of charter colleges and universities (see Berdhal and MacTaggart, 2000). Alternatively, instructors who have a desire to use the UCA case as a platform for a discussion of organizational change and innovation in higher education might begin with a brief description of organizational change frameworks and concepts (see Bibliography on the Academic Profession and Organizational Change in *Casebook I: Faculty Employment Policies*).

> *Teaching Tip:* If the participants are largely first-year graduate students, or others who may have limited knowledge of tenure systems, the instructor may choose to initiate a brief discussion of the basic tenets, and pros and cons, of tenure. This discussion will help frame the case and will provide context for later conversations about UCA's alternatives to traditional tenure-track appointments.

In each approach, it can be shown that the UCA case illustrates the complexity and challenge of leadership and decision making in the area of faculty employment and worklife in the current policy-making context.

Discussion

Plan to organize participant discussion of the University of Central Arkansas case around the following themes:

1. Organizational change, leadership, and faculty governance

2. Innovations in faculty employment

3. Emerging structures for public higher education

It is helpful to begin with a general discussion of organizational change in higher education institutions and then to deal with the specific issues of faculty employment policies and charter colleges. As noted above, a number of suggested readings on organizational change, innovations in faculty employment, and charter colleges are listed at the end of this teaching note.

Organizational Change, Leadership, and Faculty Governance

The opening segment of the discussion of this case can focus on broad organizational change issues in colleges and universities. Possible questions for this portion of the case discussion include:

- What is President Thompson trying to do at UCA?

- What are his motivations in this case?

- Would you like to go to work for President Thompson at UCA? Why?

- Is President Thompson's approach to organizational change effective? Why or why not?

Instructors can pose a range of subquestions regarding the magnitude and types of organizational change that are being proposed at UCA. These include: Are the proposed changes at UCA warranted? Are they beneficial to the institution? To students? Are these types of changes necessary at UCA? Why or why not? These subquestions can focus on the proposed changes in faculty employment and compensation or the proposed charter college concept depending on the instructors' overall goals for the case discussion.

Common Responses to Questions. In responding to the questions posed above, case discussion participants are sometimes critical and skeptical of President Thompson's personal aspirations and motivations. Responses such as, "He's trying to make the academic world look more like a business," or "The proposed changes are motivated more by personal ambition than by concern about the institution, faculty or students," are common. It is helpful to probe further into these responses to generate more specific examples of these lines of argument and to identify particular areas and issues of concern. It can also be helpful to seek a wide range of responses to the question concerning President Thompson's aspirations and motivations, not just those that are critical of Thompson's strategies and approaches.

Activity: Engage discussion participants in a brief activity at the early stages of the conversation. For example, the instructor could ask participants to imagine that they have been invited to meet with Thompson to explore the possibility of assuming an administrative position at UCA. Participants should then be given five to ten minutes to reflect individually on or discuss with two or three other individuals in the group the following questions: What questions might you ask Thompson if you were thinking about accepting an administrative post at UCA? What other questions would you ask if he invited you to pose any questions you might have of him? How would you respond if President Thompson asked if you considered yourself to be a "change agent" and why you might be attracted to an administrative position at UCA?

Teaching Tip: The composition of the participant group will likely have an impact on the perspectives and concerns expressed in this segment of the case discussion. For example, a participant group consisting mostly of senior administrators (presidents, vice presidents, provosts) might tend to bring a particular viewpoint regarding Thompson's aspirations and approaches to organizational change. Alternatively, participant groups consisting primarily of faculty or graduate students might articulate other perspectives regarding President Thompson's intentions and motivations. The instructor should try to be aware of perspectives and viewpoints that might be influenced by the particular role or position held by participants and to play the "devil's advocate" role to identify and suggest multiple perspectives on President Thompson's actions and approaches to organizational change.

The instructor can then focus more specifically on the actions and approaches of President Thompson and the UCA faculty regarding the development and potential implementation of Policy 302. Questions that the instructor might pose to participants include:

- Did President Thompson use an effective leadership approach to create change in faculty employment policy at UCA? Why or why not?

- Should Thompson be considered a visionary? Isn't this the type of bold leadership the public is seeking?

- How is he "getting away with" what he is doing at UCA?

- Why is the faculty apparently powerless to stop him?

- Could the faculty governance body have developed Policy 302 on its own?

One approach to engaging participants in a discussion of ways of introducing organizational change is to pose questions about the unique approach to change that Policy 302 represents. For example, the instructor could ask: President Thompson characterizes Policy 302 as "an experiment." Is this an effective approach to introducing organizational change? Why or why not?

Common Responses to Questions. Class participants are likely to comment that experiments should generally be introduced only after much "advance work" and research has already been conducted to ensure an idea's success and acceptance. Others may argue that only by introducing bold change with little warning, particularly when the issues involve subject matter as contentious as faculty employment policies, can a leader actually make headway; preliminary committee processes, they may argue, can be notoriously slow. The instructor should encourage participants to flesh out these various strategies and discuss the pros and cons of each.

Activity: Ask participants to discuss whether or not they think current faculty governance bodies are capable of developing and implementing a faculty employment policy such as Policy 302. Small groups of participants (two or three to a group) should be asked to speculate as to why faculty governance bodies might (or might not) be able to develop such a policy. Part of this discussion can focus on the organizational change issues discussed above. For example, participants might be asked to consider whether the implementation of Policy 302 provides actual evidence of organizational change at UCA.

Innovations in Faculty Employment

This segment of the case discussion permits participants to focus on a range of issues regarding both the content of Policy 302 and the process by which it was introduced at UCA. As a way of beginning this portion of the discussion, the instructor might ask participants to consider the role that data played as an impetus for the development of Policy 302. Specifically, what sense do participants make of the fact that institutional research indicated that students of non-tenure-track faculty at UCA did as well or better on standard assessment tests than students of tenured faculty? What does this finding mean? How should UCA respond?

The instructor can also focus on the various goals inherent in Policy 302, asking: What are the policy objectives of Policy 302? Among the goals and objectives that are noted in the case and which might emerge during this discussion are:

- Saving money

- Improving student learning outcomes

- Providing flexibility and choice to department chairs in faculty hiring

- Improving faculty recruitment and retention

- Enhancing faculty productivity

Other questions include:

- What forces sparked the development of Policy 302? Is the policy directly tied to a particular institutional problem or challenge?

- What data served as the impetus for the proposed policy change?

- What is the problem to which Policy 302 is the solution?

- Were the disagreements concerning Policy 302 more about the substance of the proposed policy or more about President Thompson's way of framing the issues and the process he used to put Policy 302 "into play"?

- What are the "big ideas" and primary goals of Policy 302? How is the policy supposed to work? Does it? Will it?

- Was President Thompson's use of Policy 302 to offer newly formulated non-tenure-track positions to two faculty who had previously been turned down for tenure likely to help or hurt the policy's overall prospects?

- What do you make of the fact that department chairs hesitate to offer Policy 302 appointments and that no faculty member has accepted such an appointment thus far?

Subquestions in this segment of the discussion could focus on the four-tiered faculty employment system that resulted from Policy 302 (tenured faculty, tenure-track faculty, "traditional" non-tenure-track faculty, and the new non-tenure-track faculty hired under Policy 302). For example, the instructor might ask participants if the resultant four-tiered faculty employment system is good for UCA.

Common Responses to Questions. Not surprisingly, the discussion of the development and implementation of Policy 302 can be quite lively and animated. Some participants might suggest that Policy 302 represents a "bold and brazen idea" or a "break with academic traditions and conventions." If and when these responses are offered, the instructor might follow up with the question: What specifically is "bold and brazen" about Policy 302 and what specific academic traditions and conventions does the new policy appear to break? Who specifically does it benefit? Are there any groups it may "harm?"

Activity: Ask class participants (in groups of two or three) to focus on the campus reaction to Policy 302. Questions to focus this exercise are: What sense do you make of the campus reaction to Policy 302? Do any particular reactions surprise you? Why or why not? What are the emerging consequences and outcomes of Policy 302? Are they good for the institution? For the faculty? For students?

Emerging Structures for Public Higher Education

The final segment of the discussion examines emerging structures for public higher education by focusing on the proposal to transform UCA into Premier Public University (PPU), a charter institution. A possible transition question to move into this portion of the discussion might be: Are there any links between Policy 302 and the charter college idea? Would a new organizational structure such as a charter college make it more or less likely that the goals inherent in Policy 302 will be achieved?

- Does the prospect of transforming UCA into Premier Public University represent a threat or an opportunity? Why?

- What aspects of institutional culture and faculty governance will help or hinder the potential adoption of the proposal to convert UCA into a charter university?

- What is unique or different about PPU that differentiates it from other higher education institutions?

Common Responses to Questions. Comments and observations regarding the proposal to transform UCA into PPU sometimes focus attention on the fundamental purposes of a university. For example, a key question that is sometimes raised is: What is our idea of a university? The proposal to create PPU generates excellent discussion about the implications and consequences of an outside party putting up a significant amount of money to further its notion of a university. Some participants are troubled by this idea. Others argue that people can leave UCA if they do not agree with the new institutional direction that is being proposed. Other arguments that are made include: Thompson and UCA appear to be trading tenure, tradition, and regulation for $100 million; Thompson and UCA are putting the institution and its faculty at risk since, according to one participant, "if you can buy and sell tenure, you can buy and sell just about anything."

The instructor may want to note at this point that the University of Central Arkansas was censured by the American Association of University Professors (AAUP) in June 2000. According to the *Chronicle of Higher Education*, this action was taken as the result of several employment disputes between former faculty members and the university. The AAUP also found fault with the university's dismissal procedures, due process guarantees, and degree of consultation with the faculty (see Leatherman and Courtney, "AAUP Censures 3 Institutions and Ends Sanctions Against 2 Others." *Chronicle of Higher Education*, June 23, 2000, p. A17.)

Activity: A good exercise to convene at this point asks participants (in groups of two or three) to consider the following questions: If you could recreate your university or college with a significant infusion of new resources and reduced regulations, what are the three major changes that you would pursue? What elements of academic and administrative culture might prevent you from actually implementing these changes? How much of what goes on in your institution takes place because "it's always been done that way" and how much is influenced by factors and forces that are beyond the institution's control? To what extent can you actually formulate and implement organizational change in your institution?

Following this exercise, a transition should then be made to the concluding segment of the case discussion which offers a summary of the case's key teaching and learning points.

Wrap-up: Learning Points and Take-Aways

The instructor can close the discussion of the UCA case by highlighting the following implications, lessons, and insights:

1. When it comes to sensitive issues of faculty employment and worklife, leadership style and the process of introducing a new initiative have an enormous impact on the degree of acceptance an idea will ultimately earn from campus constituents. Style and method may even, in some cases, play an even greater role than an idea's inherent quality in determining whether an initiative succeeds or fails.

2. Never underestimate the value of advanced planning, particularly on issues that are controversial among faculty members. Floating proposals with more than a few key advisors, and checking budgetary realities in advance, can save a leader from an onslaught of questions at sensitive moments.

3. Innovation is messy. Rarely is a unique idea or proposal to modify terms of faculty employment introduced to unanimous acclaim. More often than not, critics and skeptics will find a way to hail the superiority of current policies.

4. Resistance is not always overt. Unhappy faculty members or administrators may think up creative ways to subvert an unpopular idea, even if they do so with little fanfare.

5. Bold steps require fearless champions. An idea that seems icon-breaking and earth-shattering to academics today may very well become the norm in colleges and universities in the future.

Discussion Questions

1. Did President Thompson orchestrate an effective organizational change process as he developed Policy 302? Why or why not?

2. Is Policy 302 good for UCA? Why or why not?

3. What are the implications for faculty at UCA if new faculty begin to accept faculty employment under Policy 302? What are the implications of offering Policy 302 non-tenure-track appointments to UCA faculty who do not receive tenure?

4. Does the proposal to transform UCA into Premier Public University represent a threat or an opportunity?

Recommended Background Readings

Berdhal, Robert O., and Terrence J. MacTaggart. (2000). *Charter Colleges: Balancing Freedom and Accountability.* Boston, MA: Pioneer Institute for Public Policy Research.

Chait, Richard. (1994). "Make Us an Offer: Creating Incentives for Faculty to Forsake Tenure." *Trusteeship*, 2(1): 28–29.

Chait, Richard, and C. Ann Trower. (1998). "Build It and Who Will Come? Florida Gulf Coast University Creates a Faculty Without Tenure." *Change*, 30(5): 21–29.

Lataif, Louis. (1998). "A Realistic Alternative to Traditional Tenure." *Chronicle of Higher Education*, June 26, p. B6.

Magner, Denise K. (2000). "The Right Conditions May Lure Scholars Off the Tenure Track, Study Finds." *Chronicle of Higher Education*, March 31.

"More Money Isn't Enough to Forsake Tenure, Massachusetts Profs Say." (1999). *The Wall Street Journal*, May 25, p. A1.

O'Neill, James M. (2000). "Tenure May Be Less Vital to New Faculty." *The Philadelphia Inquirer*, March 31.

Trower, Cathy A. (1999). "The Trouble With Tenure." *National Forum*, 79(1): 24–29.

6

Teaching Note:
University of Minnesota
The Politics of Tenure Reform

The University of Minnesota case describes the series of events and dilemmas surrounding discussions of tenure reform by the Board of Regents of the University of Minnesota.

This teaching note is designed to support the instructor using this case. The questions, discussion points, and exercises provided here have proven effective in prior teaching of this case with a wide range of participant groups. As the instructor gains familiarity with this particular case, he or she will likely adapt the outline according to audience and experience.

Goals

The teaching note is based on the following instructional goals for teaching the University of Minnesota case:

- To examine the factors that lead institutions to consider tenure reform

- To consider the role of trustees and governing boards in the review and development of faculty employment policies

This teaching note was prepared for the Project on Faculty Appointments by James P. Honan, Richard P. Chait, Susan B. Kenyon, and Cheryl Sternman Rule and funded by the Pew Charitable Trusts. © 2000 by the President and Fellows of Harvard College.

- To analyze the extent to which data are used to inform policy formulation and decision making regarding tenure policy and other aspects of faculty employment

- To assess the leadership roles that various constituents (president, trustees, senior academic administrators, faculty) play in the review and development of tenure policies

Teaching Plan

The University of Minnesota case study can serve as the basis for a productive discussion of the multiple perspectives that trustees, administrators, and faculty bring to the complex and sometimes controversial topic of tenure reform. Suggested discussion questions to guide participant preparation are included at the end of this teaching note.

Teaching Tip: The instructor should attempt to adapt the teaching strategy to the composition of the class. For example, if the audience is homogeneous (mostly administrators, mostly faculty, or mostly trustees), the instructor should ask participants to identify and make sense of the perspectives of all constituents in the case, not just the perspective of constituent groups represented in the audience. Questions that can help to present and assess the multiple perspectives detailed in the case include: What does the case look like from the perspective of faculty, administrators, and trustees? What concerns do faculty, administrators, and trustees bring to the issues?

The instructor can begin the discussion of the University of Minnesota case by offering some general remarks concerning the context of tenure reform and the current policy environment. A list of Recommended Background Readings is included at the end of this teaching note. If the participant group for the case discussion consists primarily of graduate students or individuals who have not had experience as a faculty member, the instructor may wish to provide a brief overview and description of faculty tenure before engaging in a deeper discussion of the Minnesota case.

Discussion

The instructor should plan to organize discussion of the University of Minnesota case around the following themes:

1. Factors leading to a review of the tenure code
2. The role of the board of regents in tenure reform
3. Tenure reform options and analysis of tenure policies
4. The role of data and analysis in tenure reform
5. Outcomes and leadership lessons

Factors Leading to a Review of the Tenure Code

The first segment of the University of Minnesota case discussion provides participants with the opportunity to identify and assess the factors that led to the review of the tenure code.

- What led the regents to conclude that they should examine the tenure code?

- Which factors were the most influential? Why?

- Were the regents' concerns warranted? Why or why not?

Discussion participants may name some or all of the following as contributing factors:

- Regent Jean Keffeler's inquiry and Regent Thomas Reagan's reaffirmation

- President Hasselmo's November 1995 letter concerning policy issues such as tenure quotas by departments, non-tenure-track positions, decoupling compensation and tenure, locus of tenure, probationary period, and adjudicatory process

- Provost William Brody's December 1995 testimony to the regents concerning productivity, payroll, programs, and priorities

- Medical school dean Frank Cerra's legislative testimony

- $6.6 million withheld by the legislature in January 1996 and tied to tenure reform

- Shifts in the balance of power and the end of mandatory retirement

The Role of the Board of Regents in Tenure Reform

This portion of the case discussion focuses on the role that the board of regents played in tenure reform. Questions that the instructor might pose include:

- Did the regents act responsibly? Why or why not?

- Was a fight with the faculty inevitable? If so, was it a fight that had to be fought by the regents?

- What role should a board of trustees play in tenure reform, program closure, and curriculum?

- What does shared governance mean and what does it look like in practice?

Common Responses to Questions. Depending on the composition of the participant group, this segment of the case discussion will likely generate a wide range of responses, providing divergent points of view concerning the role of trustees in tenure reform. If the participant group consists primarily of trustees, it is likely that a strong case will be made that the regents acted responsibly, the fight with the faculty was inevitable and appropriate, and that the board played an appropriate role. Conversely, if the participant group consists primarily of faculty, the opposite set of arguments might be made: that the regents did not act responsibly, the fight with the faculty was unnecessary and inappropriate, and the regents did not play a proper role. The instructor should attempt to identify and discuss the varying viewpoints that the three key constituents (trustees, administrators, and faculty) brought to the discussions of tenure policy.

Activity: Convene a brief exercise around the concept of shared governance. Imagine you are an institutional leader charged with forging consensus over a divisive issue such as tenure reform. How would you go about making sure that each "side" (trustees, faculty, administrators) fully hears the concerns of the other groups? What tactics might you employ so that decisions are made in a way that acknowledges potentially conflicting perspectives and viewpoints?

Tenure Reform Options and Analysis of Tenure Policies

This segment of the case discussion should focus on a description and analysis of tenure policies and tenure reform options.

- Which stipulations of the University of Minnesota's current tenure code or faculty senate proposal were unacceptable? Why?

- Was there a win/win policy scenario in this case? If so, what was it?

Common Responses to Questions. Among the stipulations that participants will note and that the instructor should try to highlight are: university-wide locus of tenure; no layoffs of tenured faculty due to program closure, guaranteed base salary, and post-tenure review.

The Role of Data and Analysis in Tenure Reform

This section of the case discussion provides participants with an opportunity to focus specifically on the role of data and analysis in tenure reform at the University of Minnesota. The instructor can utilize the Trower and Honan selection (see Recommended Background Readings) to help inform this segment of the discussion.

Questions the instructor may choose to pose during this segment of the discussion include:

- Would any other data and analysis have made a difference in this case? (Instructors can cite examples of data and analysis that might have been used: practices elsewhere, projected faculty turnover rates, tenure probability rates, faculty productivity data, student satisfaction, and national standing/ranking of departments and institutions.)

- How might data and analysis have been used differently?

Outcomes and Leadership Lessons

The final segment of the University of Minnesota case should provide participants with a chance to make an overall assessment of the outcomes that resulted and the lessons that might be drawn about leadership.

Among the questions that the instructor might pose here are:

- What is your assessment of President Hasselmo's performance? Why did he shift ground?

- Who gained what in the end?

- What lessons have the regents learned? The president? You?

- If the faculty conceded on all the policy issues, what might the board expect management to now do differently?

- What new, but related, problems might the University of Minnesota face in the future?

At this point, the instructor may choose to distribute the two case updates, which provide information on subsequent developments in the University of Minnesota case. Among the possible questions the instructor might pose are: Do the details provided in the case updates represent a good outcome for the institution? For the faculty? Why or why not? What problems or concerns remain?

Closing Activity: One way to wrap up the case discussion would be to ask participants to describe any unusual developments or provisions with the tenure systems at their institutions. Questions to initiate this discussion might include: Does your institution offer any alternatives to tenure? Have there ever been any efforts, successful or unsuccessful, to reform the tenure system? What was the process like for you? For others? Are all constituents equally satisfied with the status quo? What are the main points of contention?

Wrap-Up: Learning Points and Take-Aways

The instructor can conclude by offering summary remarks and a review of the points raised during the discussion. Lessons and insights from the University of Minnesota case include:

1. To a certain extent, this case represents an example of an attempt at policymaking without clarification of compelling objectives. In one sense, the board of regents did not know exactly what it wanted or why. At the start of the tenure code discussions, the board of regents might have posed questions such as: What strategic objectives are we seeking to achieve? To what extent did the existing tenure code block the way? What alternatives might have helped? In fact, the board of regents was largely unable to answer the key question: What is the real problem here? This served to shift the discussion and debate from policy objectives to the distribution of power.

2. This case illustrates dilemmas inherent in attempting to make progress on a policy initiative without consensus. There was a lack of unanimity between the board of regents and the president and a certain degree of ambivalence and inconsistency within the senior management team of the university. These factors served to greatly complicate the overall situation described in the case.

3. A number of the policy discussions and debates in this case occurred without data—either local data or national data. Many constituents found themselves subjected to the "tyranny of anecdote." There was little or no data to measure or monitor policy objectives or effects, and some constituents were reckless with facts where they did exist.

4. The case highlights the important role of leadership in policy deliberations and debates. The president's role in this situation was somewhat inconsistent; his "lame-duck" status was also a factor that had an effect on the course of events.

5. This case illustrates the skill of the faculty at shaping and framing policy debates. The board of regents was on the defensive from the start; what transpired was a political, not rational, battle.

6. Throughout this case, it was nearly impossible to convene negotiations and deliberations without privacy. As a result, there was little or no capacity within the board of regents to test thinking, to float ideas, or to meet informally with faculty. Consultants had to serve more as advocates for particular positions rather than as counselors.

Discussion Questions

1. What led the board of regents to conclude that they should examine the tenure code at the University of Minnesota?

2. Were the regents' concerns warranted? Why? or Why not?

3. What role should a board play in decisions concerning reform of the tenure code, or program closure and curriculum? What does shared governance look like in practice?

4. Was a fight with the faculty inevitable? If so, was it a fight that had to be fought with the regents?

5. Was there a win/win policy scenario in this case?

6. Who gained what in the end?

Recommended Background Readings

Birnbaum, Robert. (1988). "Problems of Governance, Management, and Leadership in Academic Institutions." In *How Colleges Work* (pp. 3–29). San Francisco: Jossey-Bass.

Chait, Richard P. (1997). "Thawing the Cold War Over Tenure." *Trusteeship*, 5(9): 11–15.

Chait, Richard P. (2000). "Trustees and Professors: So Often at Odds, So Much Alike." *Chronicle of Higher Education*, August 4, p. B4.

Engstrand, Gary. (1998). "The Tenure Wars: The Battles and the Lessons." *American Behavioral Scientist*, 41(5): 607–626.

Farber, Daniel A. (1997). "The Miasma in Minnesota." *Trusteeship*, 5(3): 6–10.

Morrison, Fred L. (September 1997). "Tenure Wars: An Account of the Controversy at Minnesota." *Journal of Legal Education*, 47(3): 369–391.

Perley, James E. (1997). "Faculty and Governing Boards: Building Bridges." *Academe*, 83(5): 34–37.

"The Struggle for Tenure Reform." *The Minnesota Daily Online*. [On-line]. Available: www.daily.umn.edu/library/focus/tenure.html

Trower, Cathy A. *Tenure Snapshot*. (1996). New Pathways Working Paper, Inquiry # 2. Washington, DC: American Association for Higher Education.

Trower, Cathy A., ed. (2000). *Policies on Faculty Appointment: Standard Practices and Unusual Arrangements*. Bolton, MA: Anker.

Trower, Cathy A., and James P. Honan. (2002). "How Might Data Be Used?" In Richard P. Chait, ed., *The Questions of Tenure*. Cambridge, MA: Harvard University Press.

Case Update 1: University of Minnesota

By September 13, 1996, more than 30 percent of the University of Minnesota's faculty had signed authorization cards for a union election. The Minnesota Bureau of Mediation Services (BMS) then issued a restraining order freezing all employment conditions at the university, a move that prevented the board of regents from any further discussion or action on the tenure code revision. "If the unionizing effort is successful, it would make the university the first school of the 30 largest universities in the nation with a unionized faculty" (*Star Tribune*, September 14, 1996).

The status quo order applied to the Twin Cities campus, except the Academic Health Center (850 faculty members) and the Law School (35 faculty members), since these groups had opted out of the unit during a previous labor dispute. The cease and desist order also excluded the Crookston and Morris campuses where the faculty would have had to petition to join the union already established at Duluth for branch campuses.

On October 2, Regent Keffeler made public a letter wherein she advised the regents to withdraw their proposal and reconsider the faculty's version as well as new language that would improve the process and the ultimate product. Union leaders labeled that action "diabolical and treacherous," and as an obvious "union buster" tactic. That same day, the faculty of the AHC and the Duluth Medical School petitioned to join the Twin Cities bargaining unit, a request granted by the BMS.

Governor Arne Carlson announced that the Minnesota Commissioner for Employee Relations would form a three-member "blue-ribbon panel of distinguished Minnesotans" to examine the tenure dispute during a sixty-day cooling off period. The University of Minnesota Foundation and the Alumni Association joined the governor in asking the board of regents to back away from their proposal that could "fracture relationships" and "damage the reputation of the U."

The next week, Regents Reagan and Spence altered the regents' original proposal slightly and presented the revision to the Law School. The revised proposal retained provisions to lay off tenured professors in the event of program discontinuance (but not for "restructuring") and to cut the pay of groups of professors in academic units for "compelling reasons." The "offensive" language about faculty attitudes was removed. On October 8, over 50 percent of the Morris faculty signed collective bargaining cards "in an attempt to protect themselves from the Regents who were rumored to be preparing to pass their revised tenure code on the portions of the University who were not currently protected under the 'status quo order'" (*Register*, October 10, 1996). Faculty on the Crookston campus followed suit.

In response to the Reagan/Spence proposal for the Law School, Thomas Sullivan, dean of the school, submitted, with the president's concurrence, yet another version on October 11. His proposal, Sullivan explained, was designed to "get beyond the present impasse and get beyond brinkmanship. There is reason to believe that the positions of the parties are coming closer together. Clearly, this is an issue where more common sense must prevail. The stakes are too high." The Sullivan proposal would "build upon the portions of the proposal that the Regents and the Faculty Senate have in common." Highlights included:

- No layoffs of tenured professors unless they refuse reassignment or a financial emergency were declared.

- Across-the-board, temporary pay cuts for designated units would be permissible during a period of "financial stringency," if the faculty governing body concurred.

- Pay can be cut for poor performance, with the approval of a panel of peers.

- Displaced professors could be offered positions at other institutions, with their salaries subsidized by the University of Minnesota.

- Language about faculty members "maintaining a proper attitude" was dropped.

While both the Reagan/Spence and the Sullivan proposals were under consideration for the law school only, the faculty senate voted not to adopt Sullivan's revision because it had not undergone comprehensive review. Further, they "soundly rejected" the Reagan/Spence proposal by a vote of 121–1. The faculty wanted the regents to adopt the senate's original version of the tenure code revisions.

Referring to the tenure situation as creating a "civil war" on campus, Governor Arne Carlson, on October 30, called for a "cease-fire." Carlson urged the regents not to adopt any tenure code revisions for the law school, and asked that the faculty union "pull back its call for an election." (*Star Tribune*, October 31, 1996). The governor believed that the entire debate should be "shelved" until a new president arrived. At the same time, Representative Kelso announced that she would propose to release the $6.6 million appropriation for the Academic Health Center, which legislators had initially tied to tenure reform.

The next day, Regent Jean Keffeler tendered her resignation from the board of regents, "leaving many at the university shocked by the announcement." She stated that her individual values and beliefs about responsible governance "are inconsistent with the situation that has developed at the university" (*Minnesota Daily*, November 1, 1996). Law Professor Fred Morrison stated that her departure from the board would "remove one of the lightning rods of faculty criticism." That same day, 30 percent of the law school faculty signed cards indicating that they would join a campuswide union if one were formed on the Twin Cities campus. This process assured that no action would be taken on tenure code revision until after a union election.

In February 1997, a union vote was held. Faculty members on the Twin Cities campuses voted 692 to 666 against forming an AAUP-affiliated collective bargaining unit. A total of 1,595 faculty were eligible to vote. The close vote signaled that the story was far from over. However, union leaders must wait a full year before seeking authorization for another election.

Case Update 2: University of Minnesota

In a unanimous vote on June 13, 1997, a revised tenure code ("strongly endorsed" by President Hasselmo) was adopted for all University of Minnesota faculty with the exception of the Crookston faculty (which remained under a Status Quo Order).

According to Hasselmo, the revised tenure policy "preserved and protected the principles of academic freedom, due process, and shared governance while at the same time provided the organizational flexibility needed to meet the challenges of change" and satisfied the board's objectives for tenure code reform.

Major changes in the tenure code included:

- A system of post-tenure reviews triggered by problems with a tenured professor's performance. Under these circumstances, a committee of peers suggests methods for improvement, but if those fail, a pay reduction is possible. In cases of continued poor performance, dismissal is possible.

- Pay cuts possible. In the past, faculty salaries could be cut only if the university was in a state of declared "financial exigency." Now, a state of "financial stringency" (a less dire crisis) could trigger pay cuts, subject to approval by the faculty governing body.

- In the event of program or department elimination, the university must reassign and retrain faculty members. Professors may appeal the reassignment.

- Disciplinary actions short of dismissal. Under the old policy, the only criterion for disciplinary action to dismiss was "for cause." Now, faculty members may receive lesser sanctions such as a letter of reprimand or a salary reduction.

In addition, the new tenure code:

- Reaffirmed academic freedom

- Permitted colleges to extend the probationary period from six to nine years

- Distinguished between recurring salary guaranteed by tenure and nonrecurring, nonguaranteed augmentations to salary

In response to the board's action, faculty senate leader Virginia Gray said, "We want to get the information out to the academic community that the horrible tenure code was not passed. People don't need to fear coming to the University of Minnesota. Academic freedom is alive and well here." Of the process, Hasselmo said, "We have traveled a long and arduous course, but ultimately, I believe, the resulting tenure policy will serve the University of Minnesota well." Thomas Reagan, Chair of the Board, added, "I concur with President Hasselmo. I'm pleased the faculty, administration and the board have rallied in support of the new tenure code." But, "it was never as bad as it was painted to be, and compromise was always in the wind."